Lacock
Chippenham
Wiltshire
SN15 2NY   Tel: 01249 466814

Microscopic Life
in the
Garden

BRIAN WARD

FRANKLIN WATTS
LONDON • SYDNEY

Contents and definitions

Bacteria

Bacteria are tiny organisms, far too small to be seen without a microscope. They live just about everywhere. Bacteria may be rounded, thread-like or rod-shaped, and some of them can creep about, using waving threads called flagella. Some bacteria need oxygen to live, while others are killed by oxygen in the air.

Viruses

Viruses are even tinier than bacteria. Unlike many bacteria, viruses always have to infect a living cell if they are to grow and reproduce. They take over the whole of the workings of the cell and usually kill it as new viruses are released. This tomato plant has been infected by a virus.

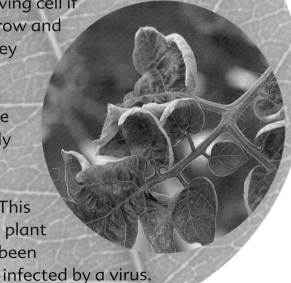

Fungi

Fungi mostly feed on dead and decaying matter. Tiny fungi called yeasts grow naturally on the skin of many types of fruit, while others are responsible for breaking down dead plant and animal material in the process of decay. Some fungi cause plant diseases.

Algae

This is a group of tiny green plants that live on the soil surface or in damp or wet places. Algae look like tiny rounded shapes or green threads, and are common in puddles, gutters and ponds.

Creepy crawlies

We share our parks and gardens with millions of insects, spiders, worms and other creepy crawlies, some of which are very tiny. They all have an important role in keeping the soil healthy and in breaking down dead and decaying materials.

The healthy garden

Tiny micro-organisms live in every park and garden. They perform many different tasks, from breaking down dead plants to preying on other bugs.

Microscopic life forms

Parks and gardens teem with microscopic creatures, many of which live in the soil where you cannot see them. Some of these creatures play an important role in keeping the soil healthy; others cause plant diseases. Bugs in the garden are very dependent on temperature and water. In mild, damp weather they grow and reproduce very quickly, so plant diseases become more common.

Microscopic life in a garden is seasonal, like the growth of the plants it contains. Micro-organisms are most active in the summer but this activity stops during the cold winter months.

Winter rest

In the cold weather in winter, the micro-organisms cannot grow and multiply as fast. The bugs stop much of their activity and most finish up deep in the soil, protected from the cold weather.

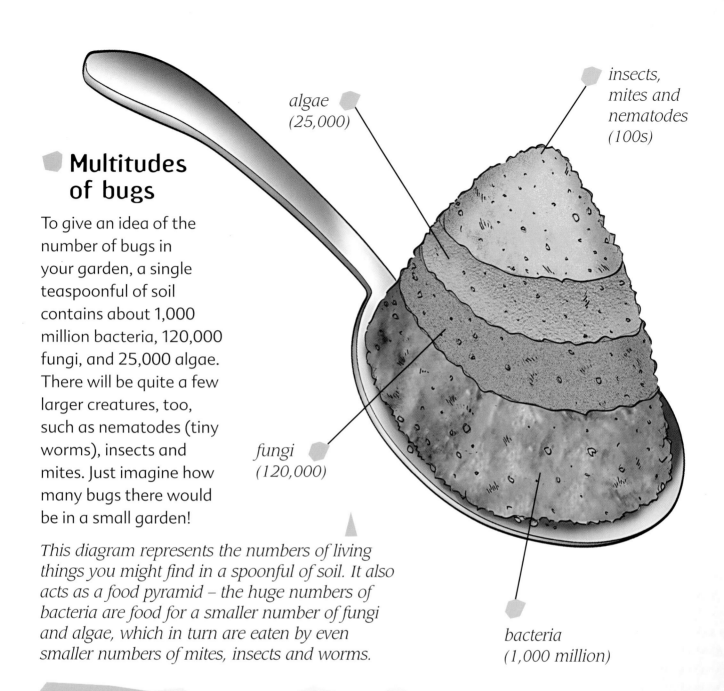

algae
(25,000)

insects,
mites and
nematodes
(100s)

Multitudes of bugs

To give an idea of the number of bugs in your garden, a single teaspoonful of soil contains about 1,000 million bacteria, 120,000 fungi, and 25,000 algae. There will be quite a few larger creatures, too, such as nematodes (tiny worms), insects and mites. Just imagine how many bugs there would be in a small garden!

This diagram represents the numbers of living things you might find in a spoonful of soil. It also acts as a food pyramid – the huge numbers of bacteria are food for a smaller number of fungi and algae, which in turn are eaten by even smaller numbers of mites, insects and worms.

fungi
(120,000)

bacteria
(1,000 million)

How many habitats?

There are lots of places where bugs can live in a garden, such as in the soil, on plants or under dead leaves. How many places, or habitats, can you find in your garden or in your local park? Draw a simple map and mark out the dry, damp, shady and wet places. Then try to work out which of the animals and plants described in this book might live in each place.

The food chain

The microscopic forms of life in parks and gardens feed on one another. This means that they are all closely linked with one another in a network called the food chain.

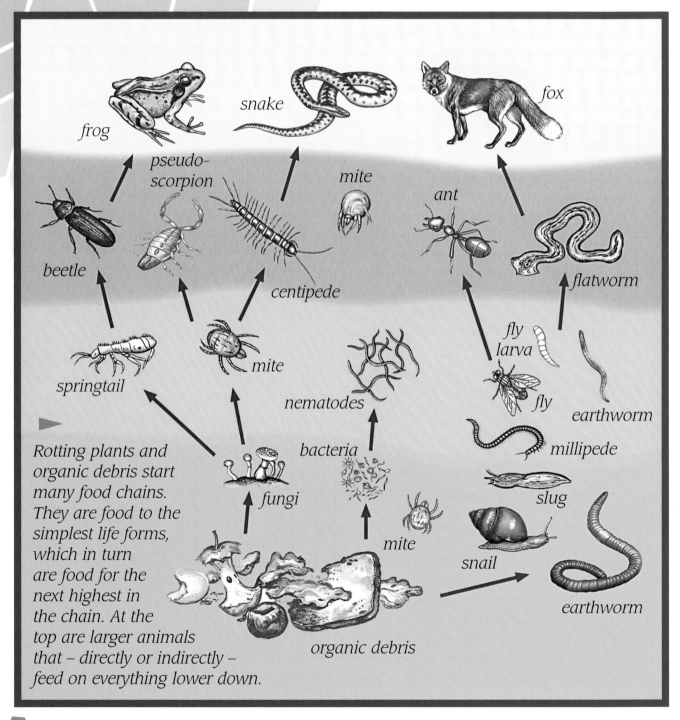

frog

snake

fox

pseudo-scorpion

mite

ant

beetle

centipede

flatworm

springtail

mite

nematodes

fly larva

fly

earthworm

millipede

bacteria

fungi

slug

mite

snail

earthworm

organic debris

Rotting plants and organic debris start many food chains. They are food to the simplest life forms, which in turn are food for the next highest in the chain. At the top are larger animals that – directly or indirectly – feed on everything lower down.

What is at the bottom of the food chain?

All garden life depends on other forms of life for food. Green plants have an important place in the food chain. They use energy from the sun to make sugars (food) in a process called photosynthesis. The plants, in turn, become food for all sorts of animals, fungi and even viruses. When plants die and decay, very simple organisms such as bacteria, soil algae and tiny fungi feed on the dead or decaying material. They break it down into simple substances called nutrients that can be absorbed easily and used to feed plants. Many small animals feed on the tiniest bugs.

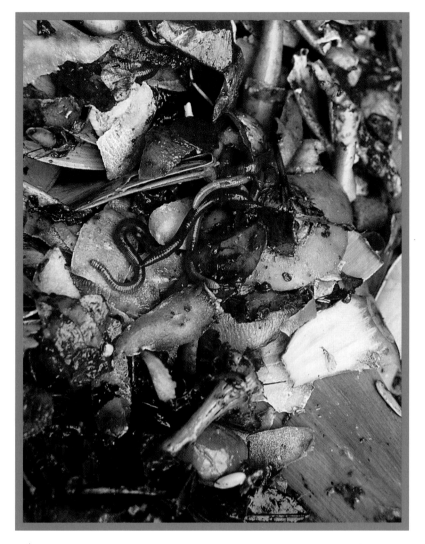

▲ *A wide range of animals find their food in organic waste, aiding the process of decay.*

Higher up the food chain

In the garden a large part of the food chain takes place deep in the soil. But you can also see examples above the soil. Leaves fallen from trees rot and are often eaten by worms before micro-organisms break down the tiny matter that is left. Plants are eaten by animals such as worms, slugs and snails, which in turn are eaten by birds and hedgehogs.

MICRO FACTS
Top of the chain

We (humans) are at the top of the food chain, because we can eat all sorts of animals and plants, while virtually nothing preys on us. When we die, our bodies can enter the food chain again through the process of decay.

Rot and decay

Fungi are one of the most important links in the food chain. These organisms are responsible for breaking down most of the plant material and dead bugs in the garden, releasing their nutrients to be used by other living organisms.

Actinomycetes are a very common organism that breaks down plant waste. Their tiny threads grow through the waste, releasing enzymes that break it down. ▼

Starting to rot

Without fungi and bacteria, our gardens and the whole countryside would be covered by a deep layer of dead plant material. But rot caused by these organisms makes it possible for all of the valuable food substances locked up in dead plant material to be returned to the soil to fertilise it.

Thread-like chains of bacteria called Actinomycetes grow through rubbish very quickly. Their main job is to attack woody plant remains. You can see these bacteria for yourself if you disturb a compost heap, where they form a powdery white layer just below the surface of the rubbish.

Fairy rings

Fungi reproduce by tiny spores. In some types, the spores are carried on structures called fruiting bodies, which we know as mushrooms. These often appear in lawns and sometimes grow in a circle called a fairy ring. The rings grow slowly from a central point, and as the fungi die off, they release nutrients. These make the grass grow more strongly, so that a green ring can be seen even when you cannot see any mushrooms.

▶
Fairy rings appear as fungi grow in a circle in the grass.

These microscopic fungi produce their spores from rounded organs that are raised above the damp surfaces on which they live. ▼

MICRO FACTS   Be careful!

Never eat wild mushrooms unless an adult has checked them and has said that they are safe to eat. Some types could make you very ill.

Plant food

Some fungi called yeasts are simply tiny single cells, but most are multi-celled and grow in thread-like strands called hyphae. They grow through the soil and cover dead plant material. The hyphae produce substances that break down the dead matter and make the food easy to absorb. As the plant rots, different types of fungi take over. The substances produced from rotting plant remains are an important source of nutrients for other green plants.

Compost and recycling

People produce huge amounts of waste, and much of this is dumped into pits called landfill sites, which is an expensive way to clear up rubbish. Fortunately, a lot of garden and household waste can be treated more sensibly, by composting.

⬡ Starting the compost heap

Composting is the way to use the natural process of rot and decay to break down garden waste into harmless substances. These can be added to the soil to help garden plants to grow better. Composting puts the food chain to work for you. It is very easy to start the process. Garden waste and vegetable waste from the home (including paper, which is made from wood) are piled up in a convenient corner of the garden, or put into a recycling or composting bin, and kept moist.

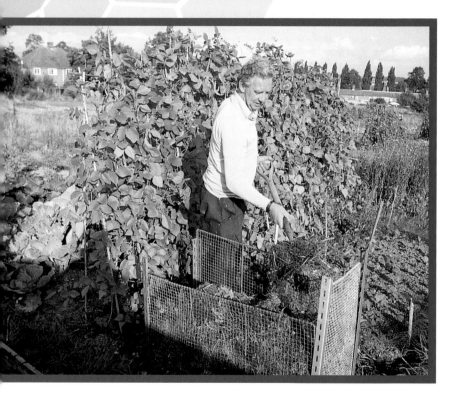

◄

Vegetable garden waste can be placed into a compost heap, where the process of decay takes place.

MICRO FACTS

What is in the compost?

There are tiny relatives of scorpions living in your compost heap! These are called pseudoscorpions. They are only a couple of millimetres long, and are very shy. They have crab-like pincers like real scorpions, but they do not have a stinger, so they are only dangerous to the tiny insects that they eat.

Breaking down the rubbish

Within a day or so, billions of bacteria and fungi get to work, breaking down the plant waste. At the same time, this process produces a lot of heat, which encourages the growth of different types of bacteria. After a few days they have done their work, and are replaced by a host of other tiny creatures that feed on the rubbish.

TRY IT YOURSELF

How does it feel?

Put a few large handfuls of fresh grass cuttings into a plastic bag with no holes in it, and close tightly with an elastic band. Feel the bag every day to see how hot it becomes. When you are finished, throw the bag away without opening it.

Inside the compost heap

Common residents eating their way through the rubbish include springtails (minute insects that jump when they are disturbed) and millions of spider-like mites. Tiny worms called nematodes, earthworms, grubs and slugs also play a part in breaking down rotting waste materials. These animals are all preyed upon by predators such as centipedes and beetles.

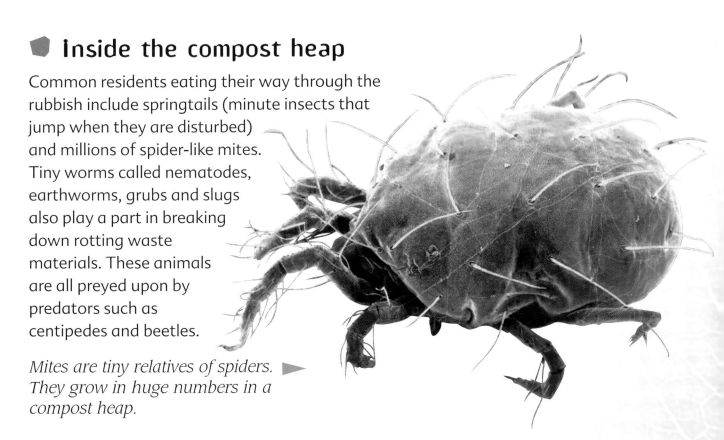

Mites are tiny relatives of spiders. They grow in huge numbers in a compost heap. ▶

A rich compost

Eventually, the waste is broken down to a harmless, but rich, compost. When spread on the garden, it helps the plants to grow well and improves the soil condition. Compost should not be made from plants that have been recently sprayed with garden chemicals. These chemicals could build up to levels that could harm other plants when the compost is spread on the garden.

Fungal enemies

Fungi can be very useful in breaking down waste, but some can also be a menace to the health of plants, and may even kill trees.

Tree killers

In the last century, almost all of the elm trees in Britain and the rest of Europe were wiped out by Dutch elm disease. This disease is caused by infestations of beetles burrowing into the bark of elm trees, allowing fungi to get in and choke the water channels. The trees are starved of food and die. Dutch elm disease is thought to have come from Asia. It is now killing elm trees in North America.

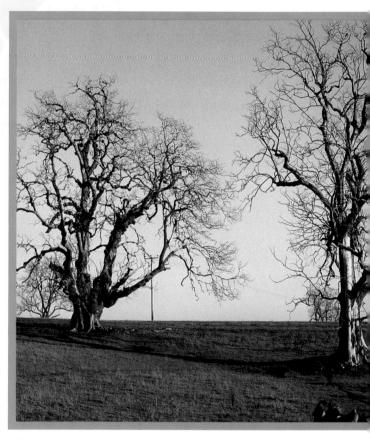

Elm trees are a rare sight since millions of them have been destroyed by fungal disease.

Another fungal disease called honey fungus is common in gardens, usually attacking trees that are very old and already diseased. The first sign of infection is clumps of yellowish mushrooms growing near the base of the tree. By the time they appear, it is too late to save the tree because tiny threads of hyphae will have already penetrated the roots and trunk.

Yellow mushrooms growing on or near a tree are a sure sign that it is being attacked by lethal honey fungus.

Rose diseases

Lots of different fungi attack other garden plants. Roses are very likely to get mildew. This produces powdery white patches on the leaves, causing them to shrivel up. Other fungi cause black patches on the leaves of roses. Similar diseases caused by fungi infect other types of plants. Many of these are of a type called rusts, which produce orange or brown stains on the leaves.

Roses are often attacked ▶ *by mildew, a fungus that produces powdery patches on the surface of the plant.*

TRY IT YOURSELF

Healthy or diseased?

Seedlings are often attacked by a fungal disease called 'damping off'. Soil fungi that cause damping off live in moist conditions. They look like tiny, fluffy grey threads and you may be able to see them moving across the soil. The fungi penetrate the stems of the seedlings and block the water channels, so the young plant becomes limp and collapses.
Fill two plant pots with compost. Sprinkle mustard and cress seeds on top and water them. Now stand one pot on the windowsill and keep it watered just enough to keep the surface moist. Seal the other pot tightly in a clear plastic bag with no holes. The seeds in both pots will sprout quickly. Look every day to see how the plants are growing. Do they look the same, or does one pot look healthier than the other? Why do you think this is?

Plant viruses

Viruses are very unusual organisms because they cannot live and reproduce on their own. Instead, they have to take over another living cell.

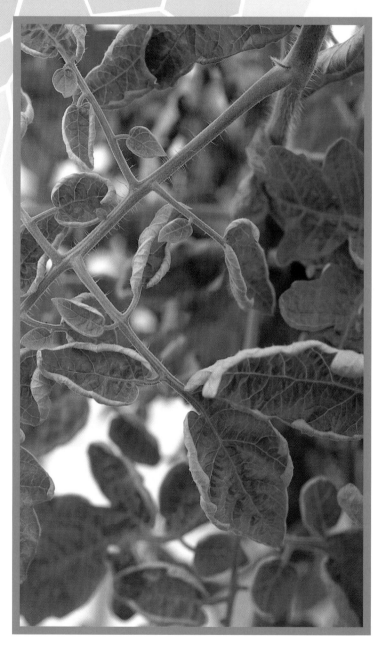

Virus infection is causing the leaves of this tomato plant to curl. The leaves will become yellow and die.

Getting into the plant

All viruses are parasites, living on other living things and harming them. They need to get inside a living cell so that they can begin to produce more viruses. They usually infect plants when plant-sucking insects such as aphids puncture the plant's surface, allowing the virus to enter a cell. Other organisms that spread viruses include nematodes, fungi and mites. Once in the plant, viruses spread rapidly. Unlike animals, plants do not have an effective immune system, so infected plants may die.

Signs of attack

When plants have been attacked by a virus, you can see yellowish patches on their leaves. Viruses often attack tomato plants, either in a greenhouse or outdoors, producing the typical yellowish patches on the leaves, which then shrivel up. Other viruses make plant cells reproduce too quickly, producing lumpy and misshapen leaves and shoots.

🛑 Virus control

It is very difficult to fight viruses because they are protected inside the plant's cells. The only way to keep virus diseases under control is to remove the infected parts of the plant and destroy them to prevent the disease from spreading. Spraying plants with insecticide can control aphids and other biting insects that help spread the virus, and reduce the extent of the infection.

MICRO FACTS

Colourful tulips

Tulips with brilliantly coloured stripes and patterns on their petals were once unusual and very expensive. It was discovered that the bright patches of colour on these tulips were caused by a virus infection that affected the way the plants developed. The virus often killed the plant. Today, modern tulips are bred with the same bright colours, but they are free from the virus.

▲ *Brightly-striped tulips like these were once produced by a virus infection.*

Friendly bugs

Many insects and other bugs threaten the health of plants in our gardens and food crops in the countryside. Highly poisonous chemicals can be used to control them, but we can also use nature's own way to combat these pests.

What is biological control?

Biological control means using natural predators to kill the bugs that damage plants instead of using poisonous chemicals, because these would kill the 'good' bugs, too. For instance, ladybirds can be used for biological control. These beetles feed on aphids or greenfly, and so do their grub-like larvae. Spraying the aphids would kill the ladybirds as well, so a new crop of aphids would soon develop.

TRY IT YOURSELF

Garden friends

In spring or summer, look out for tiny greenfly on the shoots of plants in your garden. Then look carefully for the ladybird beetles that feed on them. You may even see the greenish grubs that are the ladybird larvae, which feed even more greedily on the greenfly.

Ladybirds are familiar small beetles. They and their larvae eat huge numbers of greenfly and other pests.

Bugs by post

Most predators used to control pests are insects such as wasps, hoverflies and lacewings. Usually, they only attack a particular type of pest. Gardeners can buy these predators by mail order. They are sent out in small sealed packages that contain eggs or larvae, which are then released on the plants. Biological control is usually used in greenhouses, as the useful predators can be prevented from escaping.

'Friendly' predators can be bought by mail order and released to protect crops. This avoids the need for powerful chemical sprays.

Encouraging disease

Predators kill pests by feeding on them, but a different type of biological control can be carried out using organisms that cause disease in the bugs. It is not just insects that can be used to control pests in this way. Special cultures of bacteria can be sprayed to kill bugs. *Bacillus thuringiensis* is a poisonous bacteria that infects and kills insects, caterpillars and slugs. Fungal spores can be sprayed onto plants. The *Verticillium lecanii* fungus attacks whitefly adults and larvae, but is harmless to plants and 'good' predators.

Caterpillars infected with Bacillus ▶ *thuringiensis do not become butterflies. Instead, they become swollen with bacteria and eventually split open, releasing billions more bacteria to float in the air and infect other caterpillars.*

17

Plant pollen and fern spores

Out of doors, every breath you take contains thousands of tiny plant cells. These are either pollen grains shed from flowering plants, or spores produced by ferns.

On a warm summer's day, the air is filled with microscopic pollen grains. ▶

Floating pollen

If you brush your hand over a flower, you may find a yellowish powder coating your hand. This is pollen. The grains are almost too small to see — less than the width of a human hair — but they are often brightly coloured. They are so light that they are carried by the breeze to fertilise other flowers, so that these flowers can reproduce.

A risk to health

A single plant can sometimes produce a million pollen grains each day. When you breathe in lots of pollen grains, substances on their surface are sometimes mistaken by the body for dangerous invaders, so the body reacts against them. This can set off an allergy.

Pollen allergy

Lots of people have an allergy to plant pollen, which causes hay fever. People suffer from wheezing and runny eyes when certain plants are in flower. Grass pollen is the most common cause of hay fever, which usually occurs in early summer. Trees such as birches release their pollen in the spring and this, too, can cause allergies.

◀

Millions of pollen grains are produced on flower organs called anthers.

● Fern spores

Fern spores also float in the air. The ferns they come from do not produce flowers. Instead, they produce tiny spores on the underside of their leaf-shaped fronds and use these to reproduce. Fern spores, too, can sometimes cause allergies.

Tiny fern spores are produced in organs on the underside of the fern's leafy fronds. ▶

TRY IT YOURSELF

Look for fern spores

Find a fern — they usually grow in damp, shady corners of a garden or park — and look under one of the larger fronds. Can you see the raised bumps on it? This is where the spores are produced. Cut off the frond and lay it face up on a sheet of white paper. After a week, lift the frond carefully, and you will find an attractive pattern of dark spores on the paper. A large fern frond can produce about a million spores!

Lichens

You can sometimes see grey or yellowish patches growing on roofs or on rocks. This is lichen, and it is a very strange form of life. Lichens are not plants. They are actually a mixture of a fungus and either algae or blue-green coloured bacteria living inside it.

Tiny cells of algae live inside a fungus to produce lichen. The fungus provides shelter for the algae, which in turn produce food for the fungus.

Strange life

This odd mixture of fungus and algae or bacteria means that lichens are able to survive in places where little else can live. The fungus provides protection for the algae or bacteria, while they make food for the fungus, using sunlight. The result is a partnership between two very different forms of life, which allows lichens to live on very little nourishment. This partnership of different types of organism is called symbiosis. Lichens do not need much water, because they can absorb moisture from the air. This is why they can live in exposed and unwelcoming places.

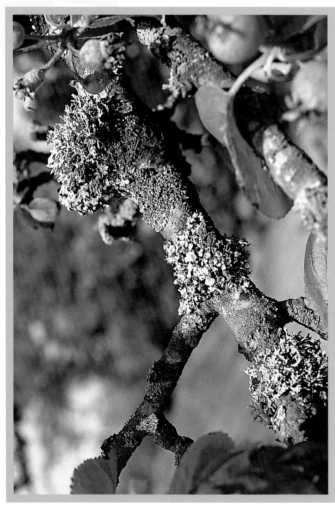

Greyish-green lichen often grows on trees in damp places. Other types grow on rocks or even on rooftops.

Reindeer moss

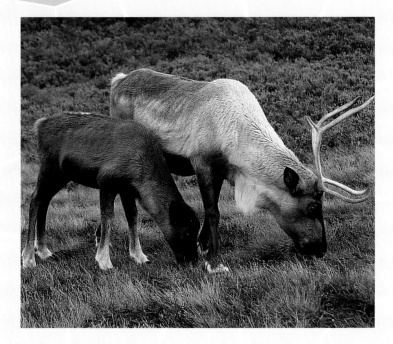

Some lichens grow into the shape of a tiny branched shrub. Lichens of this type form the main food for reindeer that live on the Arctic plains known as tundra. Look for lichens on fence posts and trees in sheltered damp spots. You are most likely to find the branched types growing among damp moss in shady woods.

Lichen is the main diet of reindeer. It is known as 'reindeer moss'.

Pure air

Lichens grow very slowly and live for many years, forming a thin crust over roofs, rocks and tree branches. Because lichens depend on moisture in the air, they are sensitive to air pollution. Some are killed more quickly than others, so scientists are often able to detect air pollution by studying the different types of lichens. In towns, only the toughest forms survive, and you can see these growing as gold or grey patches on rooftops.

Useful lichens

Lichen was once used to make dyes for clothes, but now their only common use is to make a dye called litmus. This dye is produced from lichen grown in the Netherlands for use in chemistry laboratories. It changes colour when mixed with solutions of acid or alkaline substances.

TRY IT YOURSELF

Acid or alkaline?

Ask your teacher for some strips of litmus paper. The paper will turn red when dipped into acid liquids, and blue when dipped in alkaline liquids. Try dipping strips of paper into lemon juice, vinegar, washing soda solution, dissolved washing powder and lots of other liquids to see if they are acid or alkaline.

Helpful bugs

Farmers and gardeners add fertiliser containing nitrogen to the soil to make the plants grow faster. Most of the air we breathe is made up from this colourless and harmless gas, so why does it need to be added artificially?

Gardeners often add fertilisers ▶ *containing nitrogen to the soil, to encourage plant growth.*

▲ *Bacteria growing in nodules on the roots of some plants 'fix' nitrogen from the air, as a form of natural fertiliser.*

⬢ Nitrogen from the air

Nitrogen is a chemical that encourages plant growth, but most plants cannot absorb it from the air. They take nitrogen from the soil, where it is produced when fungi and bacteria rot down dead plant material. Nitrogen is often added to the soil by gardeners in the form of chemical fertilisers. But some plants have another way of obtaining nitrogen, using 'friendly' microbes. One of these is a bacterium that lives in small swellings on the roots of plants such as peas, lupins and clover. This bacterium can 'fix' nitrogen from the air. It uses some itself, and the rest is used by the plant.

Fungal helpers

Tiny threads of a fungus called mycorrhiza grow into the roots of most trees and many other plants. These threads spread out around the plant, absorbing food substances that the plant needs but cannot take in by itself. The fungus breaks down food substances in the soil and feeds most of them back to the plant. In return, the plant supplies the fungus with the sugar it needs for growth. These fungi allow plants to grow in many places where few nutrients are available. Mycorrhiza is very important to the growth of healthy trees and plants, so if it is missing from the habitat farmers may add it to the soil.

TRY IT YOURSELF

Clover check

Find a clover plant and ask permission to dig it up. Rinse the roots in water to remove the soil. Look carefully and you will see the tiny swellings or nodules containing the nitrogen-fixing bacteria.

Mycorrhizae are fungal threads that spread out in the soil, passing food substances back to the plant roots.

Natural killers

Many other useful bacteria live in the soil, including some that can be used as biological pesticides to kill insects. There are others that contain substances from which antibiotic drugs can be made.

Life in pools and puddles

Microscopic life teems in every drop of water in the garden. This may be a puddle, a blocked gutter or a pond. Almost all forms of garden life can be found in or near water.

What is in the water?

Bacteria live anywhere, including in water. Bacterial decay is responsible for the nasty smell of stagnant water. Algae are tiny plants that also grow in huge numbers in water. They convert sunlight to sugars, using the green chlorophyll inside them. Some algae are single cells that make the water look green. Other types of algae form long green threads, which are often seen in ponds. This is known as blanket weed. Blue-green bacteria grow in similar long threads, usually in smelly, polluted water.

Billions of microscopic forms of life swarm in the layer of scum on a pond or puddle.

Aquatic animals

Tiny single-celled animals feed upon the bacteria and algae swimming or gliding in water, and they in turn are eaten by larger creatures called rotifers. Rotifers are animals that have vibrating hairs round their mouths, which create water currents to carry their prey straight into their stomachs.

Rotifers are sometimes called 'wheel animals', because of the vibrating hairs they use to catch prey, which look as if they are going round and round.

Aquatic food chain

All these tiny forms of life provide food for slightly larger animals, in an underwater food chain (see pages 6–7). Many are eaten by hydra, which are tiny animals shaped like a sea anemone. Hydra catch their prey with stinging tentacles and then stuff it into their mouths. Tiny flat worms called planaria glide about, eating a film of bacteria and algae, and larger worms burrow through the mud, feeding on dead material.

Still larger creatures, such as midges, lay eggs in the water, and their larvae hatch out and swim about. These in turn are eaten by large water insects, fish and frogs. Finally, the larger water-dwellers are themselves eaten by predators such water birds, snakes, otters and mink, which are at the top of the aquatic food chain

Tiny flatworms glide across ▷ *underwater leaves, grazing on bacteria and other small organisms.*

Watch them swim

Scoop two large spoonfuls of garden soil into a jam jar. Fill the jar with water and screw on the lid or seal it in a plastic bag to prevent airborne bugs from getting in. Leave it on the windowsill, where it will get plenty of light. Look at it carefully every day. Soon you will see green patches on the glass as algae grow. The water may turn green, too. After a while you will probably be able to see tiny creatures swimming in the water. All of these organisms will have developed from creatures, eggs and spores in the soil.

Nematodes, insects and other bugs

Lots of creepy crawlies live in the soil and cause damage to plants, but most of them play a part in keeping the garden healthy and cause us no harm.

The soil is full of tiny nematode worms. Some help the process of decay, but others cause plant diseases.

Tiny worms

Nematodes are tiny worms, up to 1 mm long, that exist in huge numbers in the soil. A few of these nematodes damage plants, but they have many other sources of food. Some eat bacteria, or suck the juices out of fungi or algae in the soil. Others attack insect pests, keeping down their numbers naturally. They play an important part in the food chain, by recycling food materials and spreading them though the soil as they move about. They are also eaten by larger predators. You could find several hundred nematodes in a single teaspoonful of garden soil, and as many as 90,000 in a rotting apple. There could be millions in a handful of material from a compost heap.

Jointed legs

Soil contains a huge number of arthropods. These are animals with jointed legs, such as insects, mites, centipedes and millipedes. You would find 100,000 or more arthropods in a square metre of garden soil, and most of these would be springtails. These tiny insects have a jumping organ folded underneath them; when disturbed they shoot it out and catapult into the air. Springtails feed on decaying material and play an important role in the breakdown of dead matter. By chewing up woody plant material they make it easier for

Springtails are very common in compost heaps, but they are also found on the surface of pools of water. They jump high into the air when disturbed.

bacteria and fungi to break down the waste, and so speed up the process of decay. Mites break down plant waste in the same way — there are hundreds of different types of mite in the soil.

TRY IT YOURSELF

What lives in the soil?

Take an empty plastic bottle and throw away the top. Make a funnel by cutting the bottle in half. Turn the neck part upside down and stand it in a cup containing a little water. Place a nylon pot scourer in the funnel and press down. Put a couple of spoonfuls of garden soil on top of the scourer (which stops the soil from falling through the funnel). Place the funnel and pot about 10 cm below the light from a reading lamp, and leave for a few hours so the heat from the bulb warms the soil. The organisms in the soil will move away from the heat, pass through the scourer and fall into the cup, where you can look at them with a magnifying glass.

light warms the soil

organisms fall into the water

organisms move away from the heat

Health hazards

Lots of fresh air out of doors is good for you, but there are some unexpected dangers in your garden.

Injuries in the garden can allow dangerous tetanus germs to enter the body. After cleaning the wound, a protective vaccination is often given.

How bacteria can infect you

Cuts and grazes always carry the risk of infection. The soil and plants in gardens and parks are covered with bacteria, and some of these are able to enter your body through cuts or splinters, causing a nasty infection. You will know that a wound is infected if it becomes red, warm and swollen. If this happens, you will need prompt medical attention. Always wash cuts or grazes thoroughly, and keep them covered until they begin to heal.

Septic wounds

Deep and dirty wounds can be particularly dangerous, because sometimes soil contains bacteria that can cause the very serious disease called tetanus. If you have a large open wound, the doctor will often give an injection to protect against tetanus. This protection will last for a long time. In many countries, people are routinely vaccinated against tetanus.

Painful plants

Stinging nettles have a microscopic means of defence. They are covered with tiny tubular hairs containing poison. When you brush against them, poison is injected through your skin, producing aching and sometimes blistery swellings that are painful for a while. Similar hairs are found on lots of garden plants. They may not sting, but many of them, such as the hairs on primroses, may cause an itchy rash.

Warning: Never eat a plant or berry from the garden unless an adult says that it is safe.

Avoiding mosquitoes

Stagnant water in an old bucket or can may be a breeding place for mosquitoes that will bite you if you are in the garden in the evening, when they are active. In some tropical parts of the world they can infect people with malaria.

The stems and leaves of nettles are covered with sharp, glassy needles that inject poison into the skin when touched.

A mosquito lays its eggs in clusters on the surface of some stagnant water.

Glossary

Actinomycete: Thread-like bacteria that often live in compost heaps.

Algae: A type of plant with a very simple cell structure.

Antibiotic: Drug that attacks bacteria and sometimes other microbes. Many antibiotics are produced by moulds living in the soil.

Arthropod: Animal with jointed legs, such as an insect, a spider or a centipede.

Bacteria: Tiny single-celled microbes that live nearly everywhere, including gardens, homes and humans. They may enter plants and cause disease. They have a tough outer coat.

Chlorophyll: Green substance present in most plants. It uses sunlight to convert other substances in the plant to sugar, which it uses as food.

Compost: Material remaining after plant matter has decayed. Compost is used to improve the structure of the soil.

Decay: Process of breakdown of dead material by microbes.

Dutch elm disease: Fungal disease that kills elm trees. It is caused when burrowing beetles allow the fungus spores through the tree bark.

Enzyme: A substance produced by living cells that helps a chemical reaction to take place.

Flagella: Thin hair-like strands found on some bacteria and other microbes, which allow the microbe to move about.

Food chain: System in which one form of life eats another. It is itself eaten by another creature further up the food chain.

Fungus: Organism that breaks down dead material and can sometimes cause disease. Most fungi are microscopic; others are large, such as mushrooms.

Habitat: The place where organisms live.

Hyphae: Tiny threads of fungus that penetrate the soil or food materials.

Larva: Young form of an animal that does not look like the adult. For example, a caterpillar is the larva of a butterfly.

Lichen: Primitive organisms that are combinations of fungi and algae or bacteria. They grow very slowly.

Litmus: Purple dye obtained from lichen, which changes colour in the presence of acids or alkalis.

Malaria: Tropical disease caused by the bite of a mosquito. It is common in parts of Africa and Asia.

Microbe (micro-organism): Microscopic organism.

Mildew: Disease of plants, particularly the leaves, caused by fungi.

Mite: Tiny spider-like animal that feeds on plants and decaying matter in the soil.

Mycorrhiza: Fungal thread that penetrates the roots of some plants, allowing the plant to absorb nutrients.

Nematode: Tiny thread-like worm that is very common in the soil and in compost heaps.

Nitrogen: Colourless gas present in the air, which helps plants to grow.

Oxygen: Colourless gas in the air we breathe.

Parasite: An animal or other living organism that feeds on another form of life.

Pesticide: Substance that kills garden pests.

Photosynthesis: The way plants use energy from the Sun to turn carbon dioxide in the air and water into food.

Planaria: Tiny flatworms, common in water and in damp soil.

Pollen: Tiny grain produced by a flower that fertilises an egg cell of the same variety of flower, so that a seed can form.

Pollution: Contamination of air or water. Factories and car exhausts cause air pollution; sewage can cause water pollution.

Predator: Form of life that feeds on other living animals.

Pseudoscorpion: Very small arthropod with pincers like a scorpion, but without a stinger.

Rust: Fungal disease that produces discoloured patches on plant leaves.

Spore: Single-celled body that is the means of reproduction for fungi, some bacteria, algae and ferns.

Springtail: Tiny insect that flips itself into the air when disturbed. They are common in the soil.

Symbiosis: Situation in which two different forms of life benefit from living together. Fungi and algae live together in symbiosis in a lichen.

Tetanus: Dangerous disease caused by bacteria living in the soil, which can enter the body through an open wound. Tetanus can be prevented by vaccination.

Virus: Very simple organism that can only grow and reproduce inside a living cell. All viruses are parasites.

Further information

The following websites contain lots of useful information about microbes and their effects on the garden:

Microbes — invisible invaders, amazing allies:
www.miamisci.org/microbes/facts18.html

Microbe Zoo:
http://commtechlab.msu.edu/sites/dlc-me/zoo

Microbe World:
www.microbeworld.org

Microbiology on-line:
www.microbiologyonline.org.uk/wom.htm

Stalking the mysterious microbe:
www.microbe.org

Why composting?
www.cfe.cornell.edu/compost/why.html

Invertebrates of the compost pile:
www.cfe.cornell.edu/compost/invertebrates.html

Soil organisms:
www.smartgardening.com/Soil_Organisms.htm

Plant viruses:
http://www-micro.msb.le.ac.uk/335/Plant.html

The living soil — arthropods:
http://soils.usda/gov/sqi/SoilBiology/arthropods.htm

Biological control of pests:
http://smartgardening.com/Biological_Pest_Control.htm

Compost biology:
http://smartgardening.com/Biology_of_Backyard_Composting.htm

Lichenland:
http://mgd.nacse.org/hyperSQL/lichenland/html/biology/meeting.html

Fun facts about fungi:
www.herb.lsa.umich.edu/kidpage

index

First published in 2003
by Franklin Watts
96 Leonard Street
LONDON EC2A 4XD

Franklin Watts Australia
45—51 Huntley Street
Alexandria
NSW 2015

© 2003 Franklin Watts

A CIP catalogue record for this
book is available from the British
Library

ISBN: 0 7496 4793 0
Printed in Hong Kong, China

Editor: Kate Banham
Designer: Joelle Wheelwright
Art direction: Peter Scoulding
Illustrations: Peter Bull
Picture research: Diana Morris
Educational consultant: Dot Jackson

Acknowledgements

The publishers would like to thank the
following for permission to reproduce
photographs in this book:
Frank Blackburn/Ecoscene: 9t. Kevin
Brown/Holt Studios: 18t. Dr. Jeremy
Burgess/SPL: 23, 27t, 29t. Nigel
Cattlin/Holt Studios: front cover tl, tr &
br, back cover tl & cr, 2b, 3t, 9, 12t,
13t, 14, 15, 16, 17t, 20b, 22b.
CNRI/SPL: 2t, 8. Dr. A.R. Crooker/
Custom Medical Stock/SPL:

front cover bl, 3b, 11. Alan & Linda
Detrick/Holt Studios: 18b. Nick
Hawkes/Ecoscene: 3c, 24t. Holt
Studios: 17b. Brian Knox/Papilio: 21.
Rosemary Mayer/Holt Studios: 4c, 4b,
7t, 22t. Phil Mitchell/Holt Studios: 10c.
Robert Pickett/Papilio: 25. Kjell
Sandved/Ecoscene: 19. Saturn
Stills/SPL: 28. David M. Schesler/SPL:
29b. Lee D. Simon/SPL: 20t.
Laura Sivell/Papilio: 12b. Sinclair
Stammers/SPL: 26. John Walsh/SPL:
24b. Robin Williams/Ecoscene: 10b.

Whilst every attempt has been made to
clear copyright, should there be any
inadvertent omission please apply in the
first instance to the publisher regarding
rectification.